Rescued Light

Rescued Light

Poems by

Geri Ann McLaughlin

Cover design by Shay Culligan

ISBN: 978-1-954353-58-9

Kelsay Books
502 South 1040 East, A-119
American Fork, Utah, 84003

For my husband, John McLaughlin—who is brave.

And for Laurel Ann and Helen—who are strong.

Acknowledgments

I want to acknowledge the Bucks County community of poets who I've been associated with for over 20 years. I especially want to acknowledge Dr. Christopher Bursk, Patricia Goodrich, Melinda Rizzo, and Cleveland Wall. Without their help, this book would not exist.

I am honored to acknowledge the publication of *Four* (Petoskey Stone Press, 2009), a chapbook by Patricia Goodrich, Melinda Rizzo, Cleveland Wall, and myself.

I gratefully acknowledge the Bucks County Poet Laureate contest for inspiration and for awarding me the runner-up privilege five times.

I also acknowledge the *Bucks County Writer* for publishing my work in some volumes.

Contents

Section One

The Story of Creation

Long ago, before the earth was awakened,
there were only water and the creatures that lived below.
Kimlana drew as I spoke.
She held the chalk and swung her arm up and down
in waves across the board.
It had been the first time she volunteered for anything
and because she had language problems
so severe it was even difficult for her
to ask to be excused,
I took her offer first.
The fish and sea creatures were happy.
So happy they grew large.
The oldest and the largest creature was Turtle.
Soon, he broke the surface of the water
with the roundness of his shell.

With eyes as round as moons,
Kimlana drew the arch in a hump across the water,
it sailed through emptiness as if it were the first line of a rainbow.
Soon, a tree sprouted and grew right in the center of the shell.
The tree had roots. The tree had branches.
Kimlana found the center of the shell and drew the trunk first.
Then, she turned the chalk on its side to shade it in.
Her roots threaded out beneath the surface
while her branches fingered sky.

Then, there was a storm. The wind howled.
The class howled with me.
The wind whooshed.
The class whooshed with me.
The wind caused the tree to sway.
The class swayed with me with arms in the air.
Eventually, the tree was blown so far over that its top branch
bent to the ground where its deepest root was buried.

Kimlana showed the top branch
and tapped a dotted line down to the root.
The class followed and touched their toes.
Then it sprang back up.
The class came up with me.
*Magically, at the sacred spot where the branch touched the
ground,*
a man sprouted.
He had arms and legs that were not rooted to the shell,
allowing him the freedom to move.
Kimlana drew a stick figure of the man,
emphasizing his little stick feet.
They slanted upward, like the quotation marks inside the quote.
He was the grandfather of all men.
And soon there was another storm.

The class howled, whooshed, and swayed
as we touched our roots on the other side.
We watched Kimlana as she created woman.
Her arms and legs.
She was the grandmother of all women.
And then, she added wings.

Dear Azaray,

In first grade
you kept a worn piece of paper
in your jacket pocket.
At recess time every day
you'd ask a teacher to read it to you.
It was the same piece of paper
you had for months,
yet, every day you'd find it
and whisk it out
as if it just arrived
and you couldn't wait to hear.

It was a letter
written to you from your
incarcerated father.
It will be important for you
to learn how to read and write.
He knew your curls.
He wanted you to know
he was thinking of you.
Remember your birthday?
I loved the balloons.

You tried to understand,
make sense of his printed words for you.
Baby Girl. Be strong. Be brave.
Make good choices.
Some days you would ask
what this word or that really meant
before you'd skip away.

Sounding Out the Words

Asheem grimaced
as he sounded out words
letter by long letter
from his fourth grade book.
Bottom lip puffed in thought,
he studied the schwa sound
and got stuck on "alone."
He worked through the vowels
and consonants all scattered on the page.
He'd been missing for a couple years
but when custody fell to his aunt
he had to come to school.

Too tall for his desk and too lanky,
he hunched over each word, touching them
like the crush of crumbs in his pocket.
It was a simple passage, and soon,
along with his knees swinging together and out,
he picked up the pace.
The syllables stuck together
and jutted out,
like the flames that
killed his twin brother
and left his mom charred and addicted.

His head was shaved.
It pushed and pulsed until he finished,
and the hush of the last word
spiraled off his breath,
and hung in the air like an ash,
undisturbed.

Curt Left Gym Class

Maybe his mother had a bad night and went down to Fourth Street.
Maybe it was because he forgot his homework again.
Maybe the other kids were giving him a rough time.
Or maybe a mid-game scream was enough to crack his memory
       into a spin of the night his dad was killed
          years ago, when he was three,
          only old enough to understand chunks
          of the murder heard from his bedroom corner.
Maybe he was choking when he asked to be excused.
Maybe the sound of the water running put him in a trance,
       and he just kept walking up four flights of stairs.
Maybe pictures and voices sharpened
       as he climbed to the top.
Maybe he crouched along the wall and shouldered the corridor
       all the way to his locker, standing like a secret facing him.
Maybe the empty arms of his coat swung
       open with the door as he climbed inside
          and clanged it closed behind.

Maybe the dark was warm and the walls tight.
Maybe he pressed into the corner and sucked his thumb a while
       until a noise startled him into the realization
          that the door was jammed.
Maybe he didn't care enough to rattle,
and only whimpered through the slots
       until he was found, shuddering and slow
          to release his own embrace.

Damone's Monsters

Warts, fangs, eyeballs, and claws
scratching through the surface of his notebook paper
ready to slash the math problems
scribbled on the opposite page.

Damone brought the monster world to life.
Usually, it happened while he should have been reading a story,
finishing his English or copying notes from the blackboard.
Warts, fangs, eyeballs, and those claws.

Sometimes, his monsters were pencil-sketched villains
who wore trench coats and hats.
They looked like men but had extra bushy features
and scars, almost as horrible as the oozing shiner
he came to school with one day, the one he never did explain.

Sometimes, his monsters were cartoon-like creatures
with scowls as mean as his own
whenever it was time to pull out his forgotten homework
and he knew he'd miss recess again.

Warts, fangs, eyeballs, and claws
that sliced open whispered storylines, names,
and swallowed screams he'd mutter
only to himself.

Vick

When I went to visit Vick
the nurse said
Good. Maybe you can get him to eat.
He was letting it sit there
while he battled blinking rocket ships
on the screen set high in the room
he shared with two other children,
a boy in a wheelchair, with his head slouched over
and a girl in bed, who couldn't even sit up.
She stared at the ceiling so hard,
you wondered what she saw.
They were both attached to hissing tubes
and dripping bags.
They were both lost in their own battles.

And here was Vick.
His Sickle Cell Anemia and the system
brought him here, two hours away from his home in the city
where his mom had no car and was expecting
another baby. It was her eighth, and according to Vick,
She don't want no more boys.
Maybe she'd win, a girl.

He wouldn't eat. I brought books to read to him.
He hadn't even learned his letters yet.
But he didn't want to try that. He looked away. I gave in.
It was a snowy day. We'd try a snowman.
I bundled him up. But it wasn't snowman snow, too icy.
So, we crunched around in it
like giants crashing out the villages beneath,
his stomping feet were winning, yet again.

And suddenly, the swing.
He asked if he could ride
in the handicapped swing for a while.
I helped him up and in.
As I pushed, we both marveled
at the stunning blue winter sky.
Up and back,
after several brilliant breaths,
and heroic moments, he said,
Teacher, sometimes I wish I could fly.

Rolf's Desk

A folded poster for his social studies project
        with articles about Kentucky half-glued down.
An old popsicle stick.
An overdue library book about snakes
        slithering in the jungle
        with scales layered in emerald patterns.
A super-hero comic book
        with kerpows and blam clouds
        banging into each other.
A stack of Pokemon cards banded together
        and carefully hidden behind his English book.
Four new pencils and bits of battered ones
        that lost in pencil fights.
His spelling book, stuffed with homework
        that was never turned in.
Three neon erasers.
His math book with half-sheets
        of timed multiplication tests shoved in.
A lunch menu schedule.
A purple crayon paper he had ripped off
        that day he added more
        of his favorite color to the sky.
A brown lunch bag, twisted tight at the top
        filled with last month's Valentines.
Three rubber bands.
The shoelace he would weave
        over and under and between his fingers
        then around his wrist to calm down.
His journal, scribbled with wishes
        about playing pro-basketball
        and flying a jet.

A pink hall-pass from the office
     dated the day his mother hurried in
     to pick him up
     and in her frantic rush, he left.

Be Nice to My Son

Mrs. Carson had a shine to her skin
rocking back and forth,
and holding her elbows
as if cradling her Julio, right there.

And she had sparkle in her eye shadow
which tried to conceal yesterday's smudged liner
and the red glaze in her whites.

She worked late every night
at the blinking corner bar
where she and Julio shared a room
and where sometimes gunfire blasted open his dreams
and sometimes even the cops showed up

as they did last year when Julio was eleven
and the police came to tell her
that he was caught stealing a car
and he'd have to go to Schuman for a while.

Julio had a chip in his front tooth
that cut into his lip when he cursed at you
and threw his desk
because he didn't do his assignment again
and had to stay after school
with her permission, if it wasn't too late.

Be nice to my son
was all she said
before turning down the hallway
into the fluorescent light
and its complex system of angled rays
buzzing in a ricochet,
with nowhere else to go.

Clarice

Clarice was the DuPont I knew.
She was in my fourth-grade classroom
and did not resemble the wealthy, white DuPonts
I had seen in the papers.

Clarice didn't own anything except
some groovy sneakers
that lit up every time
her heels touched ground.

No one would steal her money,
nor her property rights
to some obscene estate.
The FBI would never investigate
anything she laundered
and her children would not marry each other
to protect family funds.

No, Clarice's children
would inherit her eyes
and the way they shone
like threads of a morning web,
held fast, double-dutching with light.

Gabby

It never mattered that Gabby was too heavy and tall
for a seven-year-old or too shy to speak,
or that her family was too poor to afford extras,
like book fair money.
It never mattered that her pants were often too short
and rode too low in the back
exposing too much of her rear when she sat on the rug,
the place where she listened with her classmates.
It never mattered that Gabby carried the stale stench
of her parents' cigarettes either.
Or that math was too complicated for her
and she had to leave the room for that.
What mattered is that the world spun too fast for her,
and the moon rose too slow.

It never mattered that Gabby followed me too closely,
outside when everyone was swinging, chasing, and hollering.
She stood by listening.
An outside observer may not have understood
the way she was charmed.
The way she brought peace along with her, and it nestled in the air,
or how she wrote in frilly metaphors, or how her voice,
low, humble, and as solid as the river,
softened the bully, the bragger, the bold,
and the better-than-everyone,
in all of us. That's what mattered.

She was a swan, nestled on a frozen lake
maybe waiting for spring,
maybe wishing for summer,
maybe just shimmering,
aloft on whatever matters,
white frost on her feathers.

Gail

It isn't fair,
the way the road curved
or dipped or sloped
or did whatever it did
to make your car tailspin off—
away from your dad and mom
who said she knows I loved you
because you likely told her
the year we created the
Poetry and Pizza Pie Society.

It isn't fair
because you're the one
who would have hugged me hard
in your cap and gown this year.
When I saw you at the store, you beamed.
And that day at the pool, you sat with me.
And when your brother graduated fifth grade,
when you hugged me?
I adored your teenage freckles,
your eyelashes, your cheeks.

It isn't fair—
the way seasons change,
and how second graders grow into juniors.
The way moments pass and collide into each other.
And the way we can't go back—because I would.
I'd go in like a force and chase it down
and grab that life-stolen moment back
for you.

Mistakes

I never knew when Evan Johnson
would walk into math class
and slam his book down on somebody's hand
the way an angry cloud slams down its lightening in a storm.

Or when he would roll his eyes
and say that answer sucks
because he was sick and damn tired of mistakes.

I never knew when he'd have his homework
or when he'd turn around
and punch someone in a fast swat
to shut them up.

Or where he'd go when I'd call the office
and tell them Evan was on his way again,
perhaps to wander the halls and finger walls,
like a hawk who wanders solo in the sky.

I never knew when his third poor progress report
went to the office or out in the mail,
or why one day he changed.

Why he came in asking for a front-row seat
and surrounded himself with concentration
as an island gathers waves rolling into shore.

Or why he began to raise his hand
and asked for extra work,
or why almost all his answers
were suddenly correct,
until another teacher explained

that there were two Evan Johnsons
in fourth grade that year.
Hers accidentally received my poor progress notice
and my Evan was sent
her merit commendation for excellence.

I never knew what I'd tell him
if Evan ever discovered that the reward wasn't his.
Would he throw his desk or clench his face?
Or would he even care about the difference
one mistake did make?

Finding the Quotient

Fred preferred long division.
He liked the way the numbers were trapped inside little boxes
like mysteries waiting to be released.
He checkered his paper in neat, spacious rows
as if finding order in the chaos of school,
or order from the court that took him away from his mother.
Fred could locate the dividend,
and identify and divisor stuck on the outside
and dictating the number of times the problem
needed to spread itself out,
like the number of reasons why his mom was in trouble
and his anger spun haywire,
as it did yesterday when he slammed his book down onto the desk
over and over, until his eyes rolled back
and the chair fell, until the spine cracked and loosened
from the thousands of numbers spread onto pages
all sewn and bound together.
And why he couldn't stop pounding until Mrs. Hastings
wrapped her big, soft arms around him.

Fred knew how to ask himself the question.
How many times does one number go into another?
And he knew where to place the estimate, the logical guess
that propels each piece of the answer to the next row and column.
He worked out the multiplication and carried it down gently.
Then he subtracted, twitching his wrist
and scrawling his answers onto the paper.
He whispered the steps to himself,
"question, guess, multiplication, and subtraction,"
and squinted over his problems
as if it were dark and his mother was screaming,

and he continued to circle his hand
as if he were palming the floor for her needle,
as if there were some way to find it,
and hold the remainder.

Still Rashiva

Rashiva has problems, and you are no saint,
laughed her grandmother when I called to apologize for screaming
as Rashiva left school. I had discovered
she stole a bag of candy hidden in my desk
and yelled, not because of the theft, but for repeating
She spit on me! She spit on me! She spit on me!
because my saliva accidentally sprayed.

Two years later, Rashiva had grown up a little more
when I saw her at the funeral service
and she was in the choir.
In fourth grade, she had been my student,
and we made a wigwam out of sticks together
and stretched newspapers out onto the floor
to circle simple words with crayons.
We learned and worked together, using our hands.

She was still hefty; her hair was still pulled back,
and she still stared away from the center of everything;
the flowers, the eulogy,
and the people who gathered to pray and mourn.
I still felt like tapping her or taking her by the hand
as I did off the playground once, when the others got too mean.

She still held herself tall
and looked nice in her robe on the risers like the others.
But when they began to hum, belt out their voices,
and sway to praise the Lord,
Rashiva stood surrounded by the music, silent, and blank.
Maybe she didn't know the words.
She stood there through the next one and the next until the end.
For whatever reason, there she was.
She was still Rashiva, and Rashiva wouldn't sing.

33

Section Two

Our Railing

It began in the driveway where my mother toppled
while pregnant with me.
She was up in a second, with nerves
like the twisted spokes and rusted bolts
of her missed grip. She rolled, and we lived.
Whether in a key-clanging rush
or stuck in a patch with an icy shovel,
the steep incline demanded all to reach
and catch the thick brown metal in a hand.
Especially Grandma, who used to palm it
with both fists, one behind the other
in her holiday ascent.

Phlox spilled over the steps in summer,
at the mid-flight quiver, where my father bent
sweat dripping down his sideburns, tightening.
That's where we stopped to pose.
I leaned into the railing
wearing the jittery lace of my Communion dress,
prom ruffles, my wedding gown.
We all did it.
Sometimes everyone lined up in a teeter.
We chattered about nothing,
and poked at who could get a laugh,
oldest to youngest, slanted
through the front view of our house on Pheasant Drive.

The swift breath of the top overlooked the hill,
terraced with cut-out lawns stepping up.
Each railing in a line:
Flaherty's, O'Mahoney's, Gerharts', Davis' and ours.

I used to stand there, at the top,
where the metal wavered open and wide
before sliding in, before twisting,
before calling out, *I'm home!*

The TV Room

The TV room was furnished with a chair
and two couches made from plywood and cinder blocks
with holes big enough to hold a family of imaginary mice
standing ground against an ugly troll doll with long, gray hair.
They would try to battle him or else wind up the fizz in Pepsi
poured from the bottles we returned
along with the ones we collected
from the neighbor's trash for 5 cents a pop.

The cushions were foam rubber stuffed inside lime green covers
sturdy enough to serve as lake shores of the jungle swamp
where the alligators lived. And if you weren't quick on your feet,
one might snap, like Mom, when she found out
we were hopping from couch to chair to couch again.

The windows framed the corner of the room.
They were too high to see out of and too small.
Sometimes though, when our parents were sitting on the patio
enjoying the sunset, coffee, and a smoke
we climbed up onto the corner table and spied down on them.

The TV was a little black and white with large antennae ears.
It was most fun to watch on nights when Mrs. Lawrence babysat.
She would let me sit on the top of the back of the chair
and let down her hair.
I would brush her long salt and pepper strands with the white brush
until my hands smelled like her oils, her Lysol, and tomatoes.

The rug was blue. I used to finger it when I lay down
next to Mom at nap time, when she was too tired to move
and would read on the floor. I closed my eyes and rested
after Mr. Rogers, after lunch, after noon
me and mom, afloat, in the middle of the room.

High Dive

It's a small, white, plastic rectangle with rounded corners
the size of a credit card,
the perfect size to place in your mouth and bite down on
to create a high dive for walking fingers that spring up into the air
and twirl into imaginary waters below.
It used to vibrate between my teeth
which explains why it's bent,
with arcs of jagged tooth dents on each end
and the cracks with Scotch tape on the front, the masking tape on
the back
and why it doesn't vrum through my cheeks anymore.

It reads Penn Aqua Club at the top,
with blue letters faded into green.
Two tiny phrases read MEMBERSHIP to the left
and NONTRANSFERRABLE to the right
and an intricately detailed heaven's view
of miniature swimming and diving pools,
twelve hemlock bushes,
six umbrellas and trees standing out in the background.
Specks swim in both the shallow end and the darker deep end—
little dots in a picture smaller than my fingerprint.
Just like the real pool, except for the gate.
Below the picture is a line of blue rectangle
surrounding my name, GERI ANN RAUTERKUS
punched in raised capitals, complete with cracks and tape.
NO, short for number
and 160, our family membership, just beneath.

After we walked there from home, down three steep hills
and up seventy-three steps from the road,
we gave our cards to Mr. McCoy,
the old man at the gate, who stood behind his counter like St. Peter.
He used to take each one and inspect it like our souls.

Slowly, he'd add it to the little wooden slot pocket
on the wall behind him,
with all the numbers posted plain enough to see.
He was all sweat and smiles
and wore a long-sleeved buttoned shirt every day.
No matter how hot it was. It was white, like his ashen face
the day Crazy John broke loose from his house on Lynnwood.
Mr. McCoy hollered for help
in his rush to close the chain-linked door.
Crazy John huffed wide-eyed across the parking lot to the gate.
With arms spread wide,
as if he just dove wild from the high dive and landed,
he clamped his fingers on the fence and shook.
Even the names on our cards quivered.
He drooled and rattled and shouted maniacal words
as if warning us of danger, of some awful shadow out there
beyond the gate, off the edge of everything.

In a Crowd

Shuffling through faces at an amusement park crowd,
or at a concert, or waiting for the bus,
I imagine I'll find you
just as you were,
home from the Air Force, biceps too big for your shirt,
and your motorcycle, parked in your dad's driveway.
Just as you were, calling out your bedroom window at me,
that day I beeped with a few hours to split a sundae.

I imagine you were taken and given a new identity
to protect you from criminals
linked to a drug ring
you accidentally uncovered in Lansing.
You, a hero, carted away to work with the CIA.
But I'd know you, even in mirrored sunglasses,
even without Juicy Fruit gum
or dilating pupils
spilling from your sad, blue eyes
even there, waiting in line, so far from your past

that it didn't matter anymore,
how many sat at your closed casket viewing
where I ate dry air
and tried to smooth out the wrinkles in my pants
because I didn't have it in me to iron,
or to shower before my sister told me
you grabbed a gun and shot your own head.

That it didn't matter anymore,
which song was blaring from the stereo
spinning in my mind
for twenty-some years.
That it didn't matter,
how I still tug at my earlobe,

the only thing holding me down
every time I find out
I wasn't there for a friend on a bad day:
when maybe a husband walked out, or the bank called,
or someone's mother had a heart attack.
Or maybe when a friend needed a ride to the hospital,
the airport, home from work, or just to get out
as far as we go, to where
it didn't matter anymore,
what we imagine, or what we clutch.

Red

Red is a rhythm.
It's the pulsating heartbeat in samba,
the sunburnt tropical motion
of swaying hips, stepping feet, arms reaching.

Red is a cigarette
smoked before a first date,
lips smeared, cheeks brushed, nails painted
circling out a deep exhale,
the color of nipples.

Red is the stretched lip
of a woman recounting her anger,
on love and hate, on wine
it stains her teeth.

Red is a sore
on the tip of a tongue
inside the mouth
of someone who bites.

It's the color of
the skinned knees and scratched palms
of a repentant prayer
said for someone you hurt.

Stranger

One teenage morning
I grabbed the 77B into the city
instead of the school bus.
I wanted to walk sidewalks,
dodge cars, sit with the bums at Winkys
and smoke amidst the rush,
rhythm and stride of the day.

I blended in with the windows
and doors spinning round.
I wanted to be the color
of whatever wall I sat near.
To be invisible.
To disappear.

On the way home,
as the bus turned down Frankstown Rd.
I saw my mom in the traffic
driving to work.
She didn't catch me in the window,
but I watched her pass
as if I just had a glimpse of myself
in a rearview mirror
and neither of us knew.

It Wasn't You

For Beth

It wasn't you I saw slouched
with your back up against a fishing pier post
in the sand at Venice Beach
with all of your belongings in a bag,
as if you had just arrived from Pittsburgh,
fed up with everyone there.

I couldn't turn my eyes away
from this girl, her skin, the shape of her nose
and the way a thick hunk of hair
fell across her cheek, like yours.

It wasn't you and I didn't have to approach you
or think of anything to say.
I didn't have to ask if you remembered
science class in 7th grade when I clunked a book
on top of Joey Rod's head.
Or the slumber party when you announced
you liked Frank Petro
and I puked up cheese curls.
Or Bob, and the way he'd make faces
over his drum in the band.

I didn't have to ask about Kurt and Steve,
and the way they'd show up at either your house or mine
like rock stars, with a guitar and a smoke.
Or if you remembered how Ronald,
bounced down Joan Drive
with all the kids following him, ready for the next game.

It wasn't you, and I didn't have to think
about all the boys we wanted to marry
after we ran away to places like Venice Beach
to get a glimpse of the water,
the sky, the pier, and the girl who wasn't you
so far from home, I couldn't breathe.

It wasn't you that I recognized, but at that point, I knew,
I was with the wrong man at the wrong time.
It wasn't you—it was me.
I was too far from home, and it hurt.

Black Dress

It was slender with a small slit at the back
       worn with heels in its time but was fine
       with my black stockings and flats
       as I strolled the scuffed floors of
       a second-hand boutique on the Boulevard.
It was made of silk thread
       and wisped through other black dresses
       too big or too dark or too much.
It zipped up the back
       and quit low in a dip
       before coming around wide
          and alone.
It didn't need pearls
       because the white pleated sash crossing the front
          from the ribs to the hips in a slant
          was dancing with dots
          in November rain.
It didn't need a bosom.
       The neckline was proper.
       It scalloped and framed my collarbone
       and came to a point in the center
          above the pinch in my heart.
The sleeves were the cupped palms
       of an ancient woman
       who held my shoulders and walked behind me
       whispering close about posture and grace.
The only accessory it called for
       was a pocketbook with a metal ball clasp
          to snap shut my doubt.
I took it and inhaled the must.
That this was the dress to wrap up the ache
blown through my war-torn ribs.
I would leave it on
and see you off.

Music of Z

Sometimes I still focus on the buzz of a room.
The long monotone zurr of a wire, light, or refrigerator
always at work, always the same.

I listen for the z underneath the sounds in our house
to steer me out of bed when sick or into a bath when upset
or sometimes to just stand up when I don't want to,
like I did back then, on Dowd Street
when I woke up in a heap on my rug.

It was the vibration I heard,
not the click in my smoker's lung, or the thunk of my pulse,
or the man snoring downstairs.

It was the zum of my room, reminding me how walls still stand
and floors are sturdy enough to hold me, in spite of the day before
when I cut off my hair to look like a man
so I could walk past the factory and bars on Detroit Avenue
possessed in the middle of the night.

I crossed Clifton and made my way to your place on Lake
where I climbed on some rocks to peer through your window
where it was too dark to tell if you were holding her.

Maybe it was the heater, a plugged-in clock, or the outside lines
that gave me the music to notice
how the sun slanted through the window that day,
how it zig-zagged with dust.

Jane Doe

I heard it took the police a few days
        to verify your identity.
        Your purse flew from the scene
        and your license plate burned beyond recognition.
I heard it took some time, but they did it.
        They found your empty house
        and walked down the road
        to question any neighbor
        who might be home, perhaps they strolled
        as you did each day
        on a search for yourself,
        a smoke, a shot of vodka, a friend
        half-turned away like me.
They found you and identified you
        as someone besides Katie's mom,
        worried about her first menstrual cramps,
        and all that blood. Katie's mom,
        who learned about teenage Leukemia
        and where to shop for a pink punk wig
        weeks before her eyes closed
        in that sleepy, infant way,
        too heavy to look up anymore.
I heard they gave you your identity,
        one that could be verified
        in spite of the fact that you were also Robert's mom
        in spite of his sarcasm.
        As if you didn't care or mind
        the drive back and forth to the city hospital
        to treat the cancer also boiling in his glands.
        In spite of his denying you the right
        to talk to his doctor because you didn't understand.
        Even after he withdrew from his college courses
        because in spite of the fights, he was sick.
        And like Katie, he died.

It took time, but they found you.
      Even without Jeff, the man you married.
      Even without the priest, who would not convince him
      to go to the hospital, where he should have been,
      instead of dying around the house as he did.
They matched you up to your name,
      and figured that it was you
      who lived at your address
      and woke up trying
      to give away dead family jackets,
      books, and threadbare toys.
And it was you who hydroplaned across the highway
      and crashed off the road
      before a truck driver found your body in the back seat
      before he resuscitated you in the rain.
      I heard he breathed into your mouth,
      as if you were any Jane Doe.
      Like anybody would.

My Migration

I sat outside in March across from fields
pecked by giant oil beaks in Dallas.
No feathers fluttered red off trees to land in hills and moons.
My bones were muffled, and my hopes for snow were drained.

I wouldn't find my frosty breath that year
or huddle off the city bus—
or pass the morning storefronts when the alleys filled with steam.
My knuckles wouldn't slice with pain as I dug for change
with toes bent in for warmth in boots.
That year, my ears would breathe,

and listen
for something in the sky to tell me it was fine
to miss a winter once.
Nothing but the air stuck its answer under
the sideward stares of drills.

Without the sting of winter,
I did not know how to melt
or where to bloom.
And like the birds that migrate,
I left those sunken fields by June.

Route 40—Nevada

What is it about the road
and how it races through this place
that makes me want to pull off and stop
the car, stop traffic, stop everything in motion?
Just to listen to the hills and shadows.
I want to hear the gasp and gallop-
the holler and the heat waves radiating
off these dinosaur boulders,
miles of unmarred planet
so low and vast everyone flies,
no need for wings.

The Petrified Forest

In the middle of the desolate desert floor
giant hunks of log lie strewn about, for miles and miles
like broken bones turned to stone.
They were carried here and dumped by a draining sea.

Each colorful, marbleized log has a face with a shocked stare.
Some with big ogled-eyes turned inside out and sideways,
others with wrinkled, hollowed toothless mouths
opened mid-scream.
There are hundreds of slits, bruises, gashes, swollen spots,
and hideous scars telling versions of what they've seen:
The wild volcanoes, meteors, and quaking earth.
They've been thrown off mountain cliffs
and sunk into boiling lava pits.

In the silence, you can hear the crash, rush, and burn of them
and how they've lost it all,
every branch, leaf, and ounce of chlorophyll
that used to grace their powerful roots.
Ancient stone-log boulders, faces,
aging, illness, and death.
And they lie beneath these desert clouds, so light
neither mist nor shade is made
as they slip away.

San Juan Chamala's Church

At the end of a Mexican plaza,
at the tip of the Chiapas Mountains,
at a place beyond a bend in the howling sky,

San Juan Chamala's Church stands white against wild greens,
with a front door that arches in painted floral rainbows,
with a steeple trimmed in skyward blue,
with small gold-tipped domes that shimmer
as if still wet from dripping sun, since 1522.

The people bring small candles with them to pray on Sunday.
They wear clothes that flap against the hot breeze.
Bare feet make prints in yellow dirt along the way
as dust dissolves like cirrus clouds breaking across the horizon.

San Juan Chamala's Church has no windows.
There is no mass. No priest. No altar. No Bible. No pews.
The walls are lined with Catholic Saints, which are ignored.

They pray on the stone floor, which is carpeted with pine boughs,
a soft landing for their knees.
They light candles, different colors for different prayers,
propped upright in wax puddles.

The scent and flickers guide their whispered moans, rocking
through fingers and clutched faces, through walls and ceiling.
These murmurs curl up from underfoot, from vines of exhaustion

lifting off the jungle cliffs, from this spacious breadth
from this place, above any elevation.

A Reflection

For Kerrie

The first fluted echo at sunrise
      breaks a silence and awakens another call,
      from another part of the forest
      imitated, almost exactly
      and bursting forth like a voice from another decade.
Soon, the pitches and tones multiply,
      each little riff, rhythm, and note
      dangle through the leaves opening up
      to a memory of your swimming hole
      up in Ligonier, the summer before sixth grade;
chattering in the back seat of your dad's Charger,
pulling off the main road and arriving
      where other kids across the creek were jumping
      from a rope swing, propelled as high as our spirits.
I remember your pointing out fish
      and how I walked off the edge
      into the crystalline water.
      It appeared shallow enough to wade through,
      but I sank.

It was a surprise, the depth,
      and to resurface thirty years later
      with your letter at the kitchen counter
      jiggling with jokes and the memory of your voice
      calling out on our first day of fifth grade
      I know you! full blast
      like the jolt in dawn's first notes
            reverberating from home;
the hills, the streets, the pool
and that time when I fell into your swimming hole
      where we stayed all day in the dappled light
      watching clouds crisscross in reflections
            as familiar as your hand

slapping me on the arm in a feather-light laugh,
and as close as your thoughts understood:
where we stayed all day, afloat
belly-up, like beauty marks,
fixed to the face of the sky.

Grapple

Because it isn't fancy or pretty or French,
I claim the word grapple.
It works for everything it has to tackle
and wrestles damn hard for what it earns.
You can hear it after dark in feet clacking down the street
late for a bus home from working too long.
You can feel it in the sting of late feet too.
Feet too tired to kick off their shoes.
Feet so ugly and wide they might walk off without warning.

I claim grapple as mine
because the hard g makes you tighten up your abs
before the word even forms a sound in your mouth
as if you are getting ready for a fist.
And the r brings that grunt to a growl.
It's followed by the short sound;
the attention grabber, the mouth opener,
the sound infants shout at their moms when they're hungry.
It's what you yell when you stub your toe.
Then, there's the apple part. The something tangible
within reach of your grasping.

I claim grapple as my word because it stands for survival.
It is everything you've ever had to learn, really learn.
Big lessons.
The quitting school. The moving away. The failed love.
The vomit. The slap. The shattered windshield.
Lessons you didn't even ask for.
It's all-inclusive, too. We've all had to grapple with something.
And the more you know about whatever you grapple with,
the tougher you get. And the less you care,
that perhaps, it kicked your ass and left.

It's What You Do That Counts

Dad

Last year I bought myself an elbow patch
        to sew at the lower end of my quilt,
        to warm the mole at the sole of my left foot.
        The foot, the root, the base of all balance.
The elbow patch is for Dad and his limping left leg
        because he was born with it wrapped behind his neck.
        For Dad, and his left-handedness,
        and how it affected everything in our house;
        which way to turn on water,
        which way to open doors,
        and which way to look
        when a cookie disappeared off your plate.
The elbow patch is for Dad because at 73, he broke his elbow.
        He'd been climbing up the half-mile dirt hill
        leading to some new construction
        in his retirement community,
                because Big Al, his best friend
                who lived across the street, who was depressed,
                and had recently lost his wife to cancer
        wanted to investigate.
        Dad must have slipped,
        lost his footing in crumbling dirt
        on a slope where big hunks of earth fell loose.
I want my left foot to inherit his elbow
        scraping for balance against the face of that hill.
        However annoying to Mom, however painful the recovery,
        or however crazy it is to imagine two old men climbing
        some distant roadless hill, for no good reason,
        only to smash land at the bottom,
        breaking bones instead of sitting still.

Section Three

October

The leaves skitter across the road in a gust
as if they rattled out to each other
and planned their escape.
It happens every October
but I'm still shocked by the vibrant gold
twirling against gray.

That's the way it is in autumn,
when every old thought, every kiss,
every homesick call, grieving hug,
corny joke, nightmare,
and every box from every move
twists in a spiral far away.
I need to let go of yesterdays
to make room for this poem,
the book I'm reading, tomorrow's project,
and all the plans for the family.

Each leaf is a small flicker
in an ancient life
and each one snaps free,
like the small flickers that snap free from me—
forgotten names, conversations,
where I put my shoes, and which door is opened
by which jangling key.

Living with Bees

Between the roof beams and shingles, they nested that year.
I looked up at the ceiling on the third floor
and imagined them abuzz above me,
in a wing-dance, ready for spring.
It was late March.
Their supply of honey was waning.
I can't remember the name of the wildflower to watch for,
but as soon as it bloomed, the hive should have been moved.

It would have to be moved before April
to avoid leaving empty hexagons that would
attract a wax eating moth and
virtually destroy the wood
holding our roof tiles in place.
It would also have to be moved after September.
Because then, honey could ooze through
the ceiling on the inside.
March was the only time to move a hive.

We asked an expert about this.
Cohabitating with honeybees,
vivacious and vast.
Somewhat by choice,
somewhat by circumstance,
we didn't do anything.

I like to think they over-populated the hive.
Left our scene, for a big tree downstream.
I like to think that sometimes, potential problems
simply multiply in unknown layers, in hidden beams
above our lives, and like the bees, they bond together,
in an energetic breeze and veer away.

Our Ghost

The spring thaw loosens cracks in our stone wall
and Florence, the old Mennonite widow,
peeps in from the damp woods, fluttering,
around the fresh overturned garden,
poking up with dandelion puffs,
bunched in my daughter's tiny fist, a gift,
to be arranged in a blue medicine bottle
collected last autumn from her forgotten trash heap.

I place the bouquet in the window on the sink,
and the kitchen glows. Florence lingers
with the sun after hours,
tasting simmers, and my hand-sewn curtains lift,
as she inspects the seams and pattern.

She must have had long hair
that the afterworld allows to fall loose
from a tight bun and bonnet.
Her perfume, woven into the strands of willow branches,
brushes my bangs away in the breeze.

Florence swings by this time, every year
in spring, before the heat kicks in
and doors stick. She appears in the mudroom,
where she peers through
the eyes of a praying mantis.
And in the middle of the night, she sits with the owl
in the maple, outside the children's window.
Her moon-giggle hums old Haycock hymns
and as soon as the screens go in,
she marks her old front door with a Luna moth.

Alien Notes from a Four-and-a-Half-Star Hostel

Because every night Irene signed a different alias
into our registration book,
and she simply appeared,
without evidence of an arrival,
in a car packed with all her earthly belongings
including a desk, a chair, and a few pots and pans,
       I knew she was the alien who landed
       to inform us about distance,
       the relativity of it,
       being apart in space or time,
       and the way it feels
       to travel in light-years, through unknown galaxies
       suspended like molecules in stardust.
Because every time Carolyn arrived,
her hair poked out in all directions,
as if communicating a binary code in radar,
back to her homeland.
And because her teeth shone with a bluish glow,
and her face had a timeless sheen,
       I knew she was the alien who
       would arrive at a precious point of light
       and to beam
       and generate more.
Because Joe works with computers by night
with a laptop, he carries everywhere
along with a suspicious burner,
and because the ants in the sink made him shout,
I suspected he wasn't really from West Virginia.
       I knew he was the alien who
       appeared to troubleshoot our synapses
       and rewire our axons and dendrites,
       here to monitor the mercury-laden Atlantic,

A sea urchin called him from an underwater cavern
with an infrasound groan, ten octaves below
an audible human pitch.
Because Sylvia frightened the tip of my nightmare
with her telephone call
to ask for directions at 5 am,
and I coughed her away with our rules,
and because her silence spun wild
over the wires and through the black hole
I knew she was the alien who
monitors the missing;
the lost persons, forgotten books,
dropped keys, raspberries buried in ice,
and the compassion left dangling
on our missing half-star.

The Shed

A crumbling stone farmhouse can be seen
from the highway through the woods,
right at the place where someone died in a crash.
A place still cared for,
with a cross, flowers, and holiday flags.
The house is somewhere behind it,
off the highway and off the paved road,
down a hilly, gravel path.
The white stucco has a weather-worn stare.
A stare that life has chipped away for so long,
it doesn't even mind anymore.
The slate roof is buckled from rotted wood beneath
and slates have slipped one by one
down to the stone patio.
There's nothing more to it.

Except for a garden shed.
Big patches of plywood try to hold it all together,
but don't do well.
Shattered window panes and a fallen, broken door
reveal heaps of junk inside
that spills out the back and bumps into trees,
and burrows into the brush.
All the stuff of the house has crashed here.
All the projects, patio furniture, and poetry
have been stuffed into boxes
and into this shed with rakes, worms, and shovels.
The place where all the angst and worry dwell.
The dump that makes no sense,
but affects everything done and said and dreamt

unless one piece at a time is lifted and sorted,
like the hubcap leaning up against a rusted pipe,
or the board propped sideways on a stump,
or that one lidded box trapped behind
the twisted metal of a lightning rod and some chicken fence.
That box—it's in wild grass.
It's a small truth that can't be reached
without the shock of a blood-red scratch.

Out of Line

Somehow, that morning, nothing was straight.
Even the beeline curved round the petals
of the bright Spring Beauties
sprinkled in blades of grass, wet with dew
and June sunlight.
Beams broken by trees and dreams still dimly lit
in the headaches and tall reeds that swayed
in the breeze beneath clouds and a bulbous sun.
Even the needle sliver shook off the Hemlock
pierced the very wind
that ripped it from a quivering branch
that leaned against obscurity.
It was blown and slightly bent at the tip
the second at which its volatile essence
simply slipped.

Bay's Last Word

In the center of the bay,
a mile beyond civilization,
the bony remains
of a waterfowl blind still stand,
propped up on stilts
poking out of a green stump.
This land is owned by the gulls,
turtles, clams, and bright grasses
in a rustle against the hot breeze.

The slanted roof beams angle
in an exposed rib cage, blown through
like the vertical pylons
supporting its platform
so high out of the water
no one could reach the entrance,
never mind a door.

Tiny rectangular windows squint
above a face without a nose.
Short, jagged boards,
nailed into a mouth
up and down against the horizontal siding.
These boards do mend a hole,
but it's a gagged mouth,
an unheard scream,
almost covered complete—
except for a small exposure at the upper corner,
where maybe a storm tore through again
where maybe the last word was finally said.

Alliaria Petiolata

The Alliaria Petiolata is a Non-native.
Known as Garlic Mustard
this pungent wildflower was brought here from Europe in 1868
for medicinal reasons,
or perhaps to protect us all from evil.
Today, it's chest high surrounding the field at the tree line.
Maybe it doesn't understand the soil here.
Maybe it chooses not to learn
the language of the trees and grass.
Maybe it can't.
Maybe it doesn't even know what it wants anymore,
and so, it takes everything.

The Alliaria Petiolata is a Non-native Invasive.
Stalks seem proud to be left alone,
to spread wild,
to point at bees and all the insects who veer away
from their cross florets clustered at divine tips
offering nothing to birds, ants, or spiders.
The West Virginia White Butterfly is the only insect
fooled by its toxicity.
She confuses Garlic Mustard with Toothwort,
and lays her endangered eggs in its poison.

The Alliaria Petiolata is a Noxious Non-native Invasive.
It overpowers the small Spring Beauty,
steals moisture from the Wild Ginger,
taps the nutrients from the Blood Root,
and its slicing heart-shaped leaves give way
to shooting blooms
that poke at me like swords on top.

I stand at the edge of a large patch and wonder, which one am I?
Am I the one in the center, ignorant to the destructive edge?
The one that found the road's shoulder?
The one who towers over the rare white violet and steals its light?
Which one can I reach and pluck from the wet soil?
Which spearing bloom? Which part of myself can I face?
Which hurried minute? Which slurred insult? Which hasty glance?
Which spiteful thought can I uproot and toss into the creek,
to rush limp into the boulders,
whose strength is molded by tenderness;
the marsh, the mud, the moss, and the water mingling
with the last jagged leaf in the mire, before it all flutters under?

Living with Clouds

How do you hold the clouds? Or let go?
It's raining in the city.
The silver puddles and dark stone
are splotched with sleepy Sunday shadows.
Tires whish and steer my mind
to the clouds we flew through yesterday
returning from a trip to Florida
to help my husband's grieving mom.
Her clouds were high on a heatwave
and her worries were somewhat lifted
into a bit more clarity
as she began to release her grasp.
It must be so painful, the work of gathering
all those years, building them, keeping them.

It's raining in the city,
unseasonably warm, and the radiator clangs.
I'm thankful our clouds today are not
the ferocious, life-damaging swirls
thundering around the planet
leaving ruin and devastated hopes.
Clouds can be so shattering—
like the ones that tossed our patio table
through the air, that year at the farmhouse
when my first baby and I ran inside
after collecting all her outdoor toys.
We were shaken to experience the darkness
of her first hurricane winds.

It's raining in the city
and soon these clouds
will roll along like my thoughts
back to yesterday again, at the airport.

My husband and I tried plotting out
another plan for the next few years.
We are in apartment limbo right now.
His figures are a jumble I don't care about
as long as the sky is open for now
and everyone is safe
from earth-tilting storms.
We can't predict; we can only trust
that clouds will gather, and fog will lift.

Ice

Today the woods are glazed with ice,
each minuscule twig and stem
coated with clear light.
Sticks leap out in lacey patterns
against the dark trunks
celebrating their chance to shine.

The branches bend over and under each other
in tangled scribbles. Clusters poised
in difficult contortions, curved, and twisted
with mysterious poking fingers
examining the wind, the sun
and pointing to whatever's over there.
Others are marked with old leaves,
withered curls that refuse to be shaken off.

Intricate designs of darkness and frost
capture all the messy scratches of the woods today.
Thin tips extend palms.
Tiny branches tink with clarity.
Today, all of our small quirks,
all of our twitches, blinks, and stutters
are accentuated.
Anything crazy is a diamond-spun maze.
Anything complex is alight.

Edges

I sit on a bench at the Grand Canyon, far away,
while crowds of people lean out in awe of the 4,000-foot drop.
I steady my eyesight on clouds
sliding slowly across the ten miles to the other side.
I admire the mules and people packed up for a hike,
who aren't jostled by this extreme,
as my need for gradual slopes keep me settled on the bench
surrounded by the color of this place: And my thought-flashes:

I'm afraid of anything extreme.
The edge of any cliff,
the line of darkness that appears
beyond the lights from a plane,
the entrance to a tunnel or a cave.

An extreme short, short haircut.
I love the look; it's the cut I fear,
like the piercing of an ear or the skinning of a knee.
Even worse, I'm afraid of the extremes between people,
the nevers and hates. *I'll never talk to him again!*
Or *I hate you!*

I fear the abruptness of these words, the steep drop of them,
how they shut something so tight, they crack.
This is probably why I don't screw lids on well and
I leave a trail of open cabinets, drawers, and books behind me.

I could slip into a darkness no one can reach.
My voice could cause an avalanche.

Dear Loise,

You needed time.
You were so ill, recovering
from some rare muscle disease.
Your feet slid in tiny steps across the floor.
I held you up.
You moved as if you were learning how to skate,
as if the ice would shatter and leave you
on your black and purple bruises.

You needed friendship.
The hard, whole, selfish kind
that laughed loud
and adored your wool caps
and floral patchwork purses
stuffed with scary stories,
and thunderstorms of honesty.
The love of brazen questions, shrill comment,
and wizened silence.

You needed a sharp grip
to help you resist the wind
and drag you down the waterfall rapids
of your hellfire past—
a biting, kicking grip.

I collected your shoulders in my palms
and guided you through a yellow haze.
We walked to the window.
You needed new air to inhale,
breath for the wild shine in your hair.
You needed a breakthrough,
like the flight of a wild carp,
whipping in a tailspin beyond its element.

Between Friends

For Melinda

You were there when
my foot slid into a crack
between algae-covered rocks
and I found a piece of a broken dish
half-buried in the mud,
the blue and white floral design
against the muck and moss at the creek's edge,
as bright as someone familiar in a crowd.

I yanked the dish loose, rinsed it
and fingered the smooth, beveled edge.
It reminded me of Grandma's tableware
placed on lace mingled
with candlelight and the smell
of mashed potatoes.
Its missing face may have pictured
a scene like Grandma's china too;
now faded from years of trying
to remember: a horse and carriage,
a cottage surrounded by a garden,
or maybe women wearing
long ruffles and parasols—
unlike us in bare feet and torn jeans
clutching whatever's left
of the autumn sun.

You were there, and we talked
not mentioning the years
when I wasn't your friend.
I fingered it against my thumb and palm
as we studied the creek, hoping it

would serve our silence with another.
We watched the water,
how it moves, how it fumbles through the rocks,
the way it softens, how it falls and forgives.

Dear Love Bird,

Hey! Wait a minute.
Is that still you?
Perched outside my bedroom window
upon the wires tangling themselves
with my younger hopes
to the bottom of the hill,
      make a left, follow around
      to the right, up a bit
      and stop.
      Second house before the park.

You look the same
as you did twenty years ago.
Large, gray, no special markings.
What type of bird are you?

Perched outside my bedroom window
overlooking Pheasant Drive
      quietly enjoying your view.

Hey! Is that still you?
      Surviving Pittsburgh winters
      without migrating
      and coming to watch me visit home
      again
      year after year after year.

What tune is that you sing?
      Your own music is best
      though not for me.
      I can't hear the tunes you hum
      nor pick up the strum.

Hey! Is that still you?
      Watching the moon
      make awkward faces in
      all the windows on a
      star-freckled night
            holding hands.

What do you see tonight?
      I watch and wish upon your slippery feathers
      that I could swallow you whole
      and let you live inside my rib cage
where every flutter vibrates,
      and with a twang

I could give you back
all you found in me.

Count on Me

Because I've repeated every math course taken since eighth grade.
I have applied for the position to be the official counter of things.
A statistician, so that we may keep records and track the numbers
someone must need to formulate a plan or any idea.

I count the taps it takes to finish this poem,
the steps I've gone up and down today,
the shirts I folded
and figure it may be equal to the number of beans
a child ate in some remote part of the world,
or the average number of vehicles
per U.S. household.
I count to prevent myself from worrying.

Then I count the times the telephone rings in a random minute
and add the numbers of all the increasing digits dialed
in this minute
and can only estimate that the number is larger
than the worth of the diamond-and-sapphire jewelry set
given to the first lady in 2003 by the Saudi crown prince,
which I doubt she likes,
or maybe it amounts to the number of drops
trickling from the faucets over the past year
in an average Iraqi home.

And I watch the rain and calculate the number of drops
it takes to fill a puddle, and how many puddles form a pool
deep enough for a splash 7.3 inches high.
And I count the diminishing frogs,
among the one-third of the world's amphibians
that have been placed
on the Red List of Threatened Species,

including the one I saw last night
crossing a February road in the rain.
The temperature was unseasonably high,
53 degrees Fahrenheit.

I'm unqualified,
but I'd be the right one for the job,
because based on my records,
and proficiency with math,
you could count on the chance that
all my numbers prove wrong.

Grandma's Hand

I see her fingers as I age,
wrinkled, and thin enough
to spin her wedding band like a loose halo,
safely trapped by her arthritic knuckle
lest a quick gesture flings it into heaven.

With straight shoulders
and a chin tilted slightly in the air
Grandma graced our congregation
of hand-me-downs, dirty knees
and with any luck, a root beer float.

Her hands,
dotted with age spots and webby veins
were more intricate than the designs woven
into her lace tablecloth spread wide
with family cheeks, clanging forks, and laughter.

I picture them tapping rhythms
onto the arms of her chair
as if lost in the thrum of everyone.
Lost, as I am in my nightmare sometimes
when I turn left off of Frankstown Rd.

and onto the rumbling cobblestone hill
that spirals down the rooftops of Wilkinsburg.
Lost, in search of her house on Ellis Street.

Double Arches

For Dr. Mo

The Double Arches stand in the desert sun like us,
two old friends posed differently
with shadows and cracks that twist and dip
through wide-open gaps for air,
easy access for silences and for each other.

Double Arches reminds me of our twos,
our two best-friend hands held and swinging together
through warm, sloshing puddles at the pool.
Our two heads asleep in a pup tent at Camp Redwing
when we talked about running away.
We'd follow the railroad tracks until a rumbling train
would arrive just slow enough for us to grab hold
and jump aboard. Who cares where it was headed?

Two caramel creams with the white stuff eaten away
and plugging them into our little eyes—candy glasses
to squint through, out at the sun. And how our years grew
into too many and too much.

Two scoops of ice cream in a Peanut Buster Parfait,
time for two cigarettes, and two bottles of wine,
the two ferries we boarded together as we traveled
over two European seas when we turned thirty
and you took two weeks off to lead me around.

One arch stands wider and taller like a bridge, like you.
The other stands a little off to the left and back,
it looks more afraid, like me, but follows.
The way I've followed your focus on whatever comes next.
Through city streets, up high trails, through mountains,

down school corridors and over the bridges
I wouldn't have found alone,
even halfway up the Blarney Stone Castle
the year I found myself too afraid to go farther.

And on our last visit, I followed you down the Colorado River,
and through a cave behind Rifle Falls
because the front was too steep for me.
These ancient arches stand hollowed out together.
You can climb right through and into them,
and they rise into the sky.
Double Arches are the giant rock remains of a second chance,
and the sheer red strength of all the seconds we still have.

Section Four

Tricycle Rescue

For my quilt, I found a red rose
and sewed it at my right foot
to remind me of a day
when I was three.

A rose,
as red as my tricycle
on Rose Avenue that day
and as loud as Ronnie Byers

who ran crazy out of his house
jumping hedges to stop the truck driver
backing right over me.

A rose as big as the pipes
underneath the truck
that transfixed me like twisted miniature
steel mill furnaces
coughing up smoke

as I sang and drove my tricycle
deep in play, pretend-driving right through
the Squirrel Hill tunnel.

That rose is for Mom,
for her grip and sobbing relief.

Sisters, Circles, Dots

Somewhere near the center of my quilt
      I'll sew two navy circles, sisters of cloth
      with white polka dots to remind me of my sister, Margie,
      and the dress she wore to my wedding.
The night before, I dreamt of her in the same dress.
      And there she was in the morning,
      bouncing into the sunlight,
      glowing with smiles and wearing my dream.
      She brought me something old.
      One of Grandma's doilies to hold wrapped
      around the handle of my bouquet.
      Something as old as sisters could recall,
      Grandma's house, flowers, and those dots
      that spun around her, pretty,
      like the buttercups we used to pluck
      and spin under our chins to test if we liked butter.
Maybe Margie had mentioned her dress
      and that's why I dreamed of her wearing it.
      Or maybe I just knew,
      like the way I knew where to swim
      when she pointed to me underwater
      and showed me where to look for a penny
      bouncing on the pool floor.
      And the way she knew
      when to call me on the phone and take me in,
      because life was too hard for me sometimes.
      And she knew how to help me find a job,
      a place to rent, and the courage to start reconnecting.
Maybe she had described it to me before my dream,
      or maybe, like a sister, I knew she would wear polka dots
      to match her polka dancing smiles for me that day.
      Those dots spun around her like cartwheels
      down our front lawn, filled with dandelions and daisies.

Sometimes they spun the other way,
as sisters do when they scratch and snarl
over games, toys, and a stolen sweater.
Red bickering swirls of anger colliding in the universe
only to disappear between deep breaths, shared losses,
distance, weddings, and time marking the spot
with two circles and Margie's polka dots.

Your Handed-Down Rug

For Nana

This dirt is yours
after a poor hand at poker
and a high ball for lunch
when you'd catch me at home
skipping school.

The chain of flowers
edging the fringe is faded
and worn with mashed potatoes, holiday spills,
dog hair, and a day when you gave me your watch.

It is still, like that silence
after you made another bad joke;
hurting someone around
but you never meant it that way.

The warmth in the red design
feels like your tap on my arm.
The way you'd elbow me and say
Don't tell your mom.
Shoulders hunched over rose-tinted glasses
when no one would listen.

I remember your chair, your stale pink mints,
and when we didn't say much
as we'd rock.
You never had to be right,
and never said I was wrong
to land broken
with swollen eyes, palming your rug.
My sunken cheek curled up
pressing into the vines
and leaves spun around.

Pineapple Fountains

The woman who stitched the design
on this table runner knew pineapples.
Her periwinkle pineapple checkers fountain up
into a stack of bright petals.
Her stitches are not perfect, but confident.
She knew that it matters,
the work of each stitch, simple or trying,
matters the way each torn section of leaf
matters to each ant walking through grass.
She loved this design; it's obvious
by the way she stacked the flowers too high.
She probably laughed as she did, unabashed,
daring the top one to touch
closer to the center than ever before.
She wasn't vain, just playful.
Her joy sprung up.

The woman who stitched this design
would have placed one pineapple
centered on this runner.
A nice, ripe pineapple with leaves
pointing upward, a bunch of warm rays
off the top of its oblong base.

A slightly tilted pineapple to welcome everyone
who came to visit, which happened often
because anyone who knew such balance,
also understood the work and nature
of fountains, and pineapples, and people.
How each one matters. And how we teeter—
how even a line of ants
will curve around something, sure enough
to go their own way.

Unfinished Red Roses

Who would buy this stained, unfinished,
red-threaded sampler
of two large bouquets for $3.50?
Me.
I pulled it from a pile of pretty pastels
at the antique shop because the muslin is old and soft
and the woman drew her flowers with a pencil, freehand.
She experimented with running stitches and linking chains
in two swift bouquets of calla lilies and unfinished roses.
Bold red stitches against white
like berries and cardinals perched in the snow.
The eye is steered in twists over lilies sewn
with end-to-end stitches
the way days can line up in a row,
then the eye follows to the heart-shaped leaves done in doubles,
and roses made shorter and tighter, thicker
until the last stitch falls off, half-done.

This sampler was sewn by a mom, like me,
who can't seem to get anything done,
who cooks in a mess and waits to clean
and who lets her kids play outside
alone for too long
kicking and stomping in the rain.
This mom will dance with red passion
or dive into the pond
and she doesn't sit still
unless to sigh with relief
at the end of an ordinary day.

On the reverse side, the knots tie and ends crossover
in wild arrays of freedom
like my daughter's hair hung too long over one eye.
These red threads on the back
touch in tangles too, like the blankets
I find my other daughter
wrinkled up in when I have to wake her,
and all of us
from our unfinished dreams.

Tearstained Satin

Tiny bits of blue satin,
some with a bit of white ruffle
will go on the outer edge of the quilt I'll make.
They will spill over the side of my bed
and hang above the floor, like pearls dangling
from a loose string.

These satin swatches will be cut into broken pieces
to remind me of the broken day
I yelled at my two-year-old Helen,
probably for crying again
because she cried a lot
and sometimes,
it threw me into a chaotic rage
even though I tried to control myself,
even though the after-guilt would crush us
even though no one deserved a screaming mom
who made her baby take off the Cinderella dress-up dress
to bring out to the big trash can
so she could throw it all away,
the dress, the tension, the tantrums,
and the too much of everything
except for tranquility.

I want to remember that blue satin
and try to stitch it back together
because we both still remember that day,
and the tearstained dress,
even though we don't like to,
even though I held my ten-year-old Helen today,
smooth and soft, and apologized again.
And even though it hurt,
she doesn't want another one.
Not another dress. Or another mom.

Irish Ferry

A large family boarded the ferry
as if it would take weeks
to cross the Irish Sea from an English shore.

They walked inside together.
The women wore laughter and smudgy children,
the men wore fiddles slung as loosely on their backs
as their curls and clatter.

With a list in hand,
each child set out
in a search of items for a scavenger hunt.
They sniffed their surroundings.
They spoke to strangers,
asking for paperclips, a magnet, an old ticket stub,
or perhaps a piece of candy?
With quick eyes, they crawled under tables
and picked up lint as if it were gold.

One boy approached me and asked if I had a straight pin.
I searched my purse.
I fumbled through hairspray and lipstick,
some mints and cash.
My life wasn't empty.
But there, far from shore,
with a child raised on this music and clamor,
I hunted down to the thread in my socks,
and found only the point.
I needed more.

Two Pansies in a Pot

These old napkins match exactly.
Stitched on worn, browned linen,
I imagine they were embroidered by two old friends.
Each portrays two bright pansies with clashing buds
blooming in bold red and pink out of a blue checkered pot.

The outside edge of every petal highlights
inward lines, close together,
like the minute dashes on a ticking clock.
The center of each encircle a black and orange star
minuscule lines and dots, lines and dots,
surrounding petals.
Nine painstakingly perfect olive-shaped buds
poke above and behind the twin pansies.
Tangerine, lavender, and periwinkle,
all organized and centered in clusters,
each adorned with a pimento red drop.
Black stems match black veins on lime leaves.
And they match the one line of black waves
these crazy pots are balanced upon.
The black waves are mirrored by the trim.
The outside edges zig-zag in
coffee-colored mountains,
attached by dashes again.

The lines, dots, and waves of mix-matched color
repeat throughout this design.
I imagine the design was created by best friends,
who knew to leave something easy
so, they left the top empty, silent and still,
light as a cloud for these
two pansies in a pot,
one for understanding comfort,
the other, for comfort, understood.

Wind Breaker

I climbed the stairs from the dank basement
where puddles still lingered from the last storm,
puddles, sprinkled with flung flecks of foaming kitty litter,
where spiders scuttle for cover under the rags
I threw to the floor from the kitchen
waiting for the next load.
On the way up, I saw it.
That bright orange windbreaker jacket,
the one I wore on my runs at dusk
through the curved-hill roads off Richlandtown.
It was hung by the hood on a nail.

I wanted to remember to pack it
for my daughter who bicycles the streets of the city
late at night, home from work.
She could use this, I thought.
I passed it, on the stairs, on my way
to some place, I don't know,
maybe to the kitchen with laundry in hand,
maybe to the car, off to work.
Maybe to get the whistling kettle.
Only my dream can understand
why, where, or how that jacket appeared.
Or where it ended up, in a box or a bag on our move,
that left John with a backache for weeks
and me with these dreams
of forgotten, every day trivial
flashes of color whipped through black.
Questions in search of my sleep.
I don't even care about that jacket.

Who knows about memories and dreams?
Who knows why those basement stairs and bright jackets
blew through the wavering lines of conscious and sub?
Who knows why I dreamt of remembering something
I lost and forgot and needed for my daughter?
Maybe that's the way it is.
I'm a mother and daughter
just drifting our way
from the web-riddled wrinkles of a brain
no one really understands yet.
Just stars, planets, molecules, and atoms
lighting up, bumping, and breaking away
the magnetic winds of our past.

What We Hold

I was surprised to spot two fawns
embroidered on a table runner
in brown stitches among the decorated, ornate
flowers, French knots and twists.

I was grateful to see an image of anything
besides flowers. Deer. Straightforward and simple
as if they had just walked out of the woods,
leaping in play the way my girls did

when they climbed the magnolia,
took turns hiding from caterpillars,
or dressed in a quest to conquer monsters
in shouts, in the grass, in mud.

The deer are pictured close-up, necks embraced,
both profiles. Blue eyes peer downward,
in another world, with spring green vines
and red buds swung under

entwined. I imagine this in a log cabin lodge
in the woods where the fire crackles
and April birds holler and chatter.
Stitched by a woman, a natural mother.

It stunned me to examine the brown fur.
Each shadow and tuft, perfectly straight
like the stun at the sight of a bald eagle or bear
or of finding these flashbacks

to when my girls were toddlers
bobbing on rocks in the creek to catch fish in a bucket
or the leopard frog, Hoppy, just to hold him awhile
cheek to rubbery flesh, in their own caress.

A Turtle

After twisting deep
through silent waves,
a turtle emerged from the creek.
      Dragging herself ashore,
        she lumbered through the grass,
        leather-thick.
Sharp, her hook protruded
      beneath warm eyes.
She nosed along to the rhythm
      printed on her shell,
        as if she landed here from
        another age.
like a trunk,
      all packed
      with muscle, eggs,
      and snap.

My Quilt

I'm going to stitch together a quilt this summer
when I have time to think about colors and patterns.
It won't match. It won't be pretty.
It may get loud at the corners or have frustrating seams
with soft patches of pumpkin orange orbiting
in no organized pattern throughout, to remind me of Dad
and that orange sweater he wore for years around the house.
So old, he wore holes through the elbows.

I want to accent it with black fabric printed with pink roses too.
Bright petals unfurling like the folds of Grandma's hair
when she wore it up.
I search for the smell
of roses and tea and potatoes steaming down the long corridor
where she kept her metal fold-up trays.
The ones we would use for dinner.
The ones with big, pink roses patched here and there
in random designs as if playing Ring Around the Rosie
falling down into the dress she gave me special,
wrapped in tissue paper to match.
That was the year Michele was born.
My dress was black with big pink roses
prancing outside on my first day of school
where I posed for the camera.
All curls, squinting into the sun.

My quilt will have pieces of the pink bathing suit
I wore when I was little too.
The one that earned me the nickname "Pinky."
And blue silk ribbons I won at the meets.

I'll put white nylon sections near the center,
near the head, near the ankles, and anywhere that might ache.
Even on John's side.

105

To remind me of Mom and her nurse uniform.
Maybe even barky brown furry parts, in honor of Puppet,
the dog she had to put down.

The whole quilt needs to be life-wrinkled and carefree.
Captured memories spun together to cradle more than me.

Our Light

For Helen

When all was frozen, white on fields
and silence overtook the stream,
you arrived, as estimated.

Healthy, wrinkled,
and as plump as the sky
ablaze like that sunset we witnessed together

a few random Wednesdays ago.
You are those unimaginable colors
in the midst of mundane.

Brilliant fires alive with pink
and soft lavenders landing
the way your cheek settles into

one of your hugs.
You have this music,
the glorious shine

when we're all run down, too cold,
busy or sick.
You are a sky dance

free for everyone,
arriving daily.
You are the fresh hope,

the hush.

You

For Laurel

are a breathless tink.
A sunrise with a trillion tiny icicles
glimmering
along every branch,
every sliver, every tip in the forest.
Each crazy diamond
dangles
stunned in a silent maze,
stilled in its own moments
layer after crystal lace-layer.
Wild, random scrabbly sticks wear pearly sleeves
droplets
of frozen sun.
Ice-glinting beauty that
halts
the way your complexity does.
Grounded,
your strong root
withstands wind shatter.
You engage and explore,
bewildered, brilliant.
You are shock-frozen morning tree tips
redirecting radiance.
You are
illuminated, elated light.

The Mason Jar

For John

I've kept the fifties kitchen curtain fabric
in a wooden box under my bed for seven years.
I didn't know what to do with it
when my sister gave it to me,
a leftover yard from her mother-in-law up in Michigan.
I didn't know what to make of it either,
big mason jars filled with bright foods
labeled mushrooms, oranges, pears on a white background
interlaced with brown, orange, and yellow checkerboards.

This pattern is like a summer morning
in a farmhouse kitchen
where a woman wears an apron
as she stirs, simmers, seasons.
A woman with too much to do,
a drop of sweat behind her ear,
ready to swat and kill the next fly,
or anything in her way.
I'm not that woman.
But I kept the fabric because almost everyone
wants to concoct, dice, steam, and mince
the aromas of family into a jar
potent enough to ward off any danger,
any illness or trouble.

That's why I chose to use this fabric for my quilt,
and why it reminds me of my husband, John.
He's the cook who loves a farmhouse kitchen.
He simmers tomatoes, picks berries, plans ahead
for winter nights when we're crazed with work

on too little sunlight, overwrought with ice and tired eyes.
On nights when a damp soreness can't be shaken
and we need a quilt with summer morning mason jars
sewn in the middle, on the edge, and at the foot.

That's why in one mason jar on John's side of the bed,
I deliberately chose to sew a patch of black fabric
with a star radiating in perfect golden lines.
It's aglow for dark, frozen days.
I'm not a farmhouse woman in a kitchen.
But I'll take her curtains
and wrap us under those mason jars
to breathe in all of our well-traveled, rescued light.

About the Author

Geri Ann McLaughlin studied poetry and creative writing while earning her degree. This included classes at Duquesne University, University of Pittsburgh, and a 5-credit graduate class in Dublin, Ireland, at the Parnell Writing Center in the summer of 1995.

After graduating from the University of Pittsburgh with a BS in Elementary Education in 1989, she moved to Delaware to begin her teaching career. There, she taught 4th grade for five years. Then, after getting married, she moved to Bucks County, PA where she currently teaches. Recently, she also earned a Master's in Early Childhood Literacy from Wilkes University and a Master's Teaching Certificate in Gifted and Talented Education from Millersville University. All of which inform her poetry.

She and her husband, John, raised their daughters, Laurel Ann and Helen, as they managed and resided in the Weisel Hostel in Lake Nockamixon State Park. Now, their daughters are young adults. John and Geri Ann live in Lansdale, PA, with their dog, Flynn.